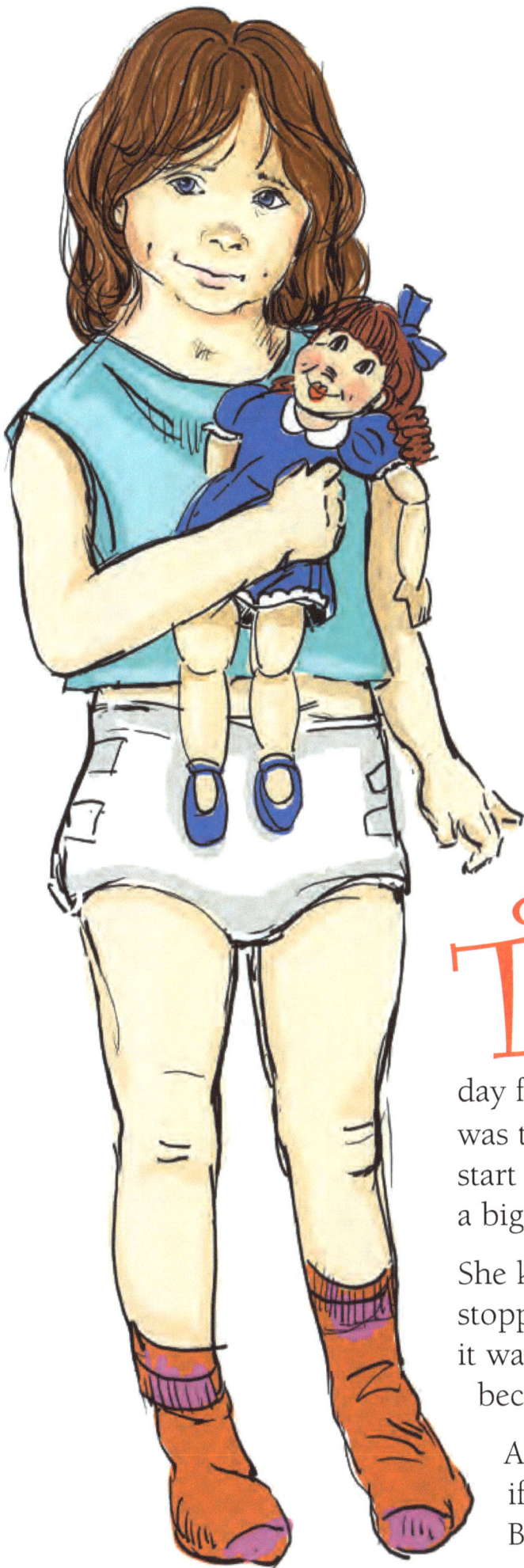

Today was a very special day for Alexa, because THIS was the day she was going to start potty training. And what a big decision this was!

She knew that once she stopped wearing diapers, it was the start of her becoming a big girl.

Alexa wasn't quite sure if she was ready for this BIG CHANGE!

Alexa's Mommy had a book on "Potty Training Your Child," and Alexa liked looking at the pictures of the little kids sitting on their potties.

"Oh, how grown up they look," thought Alexa.

"Will I be grown up like that, too?"

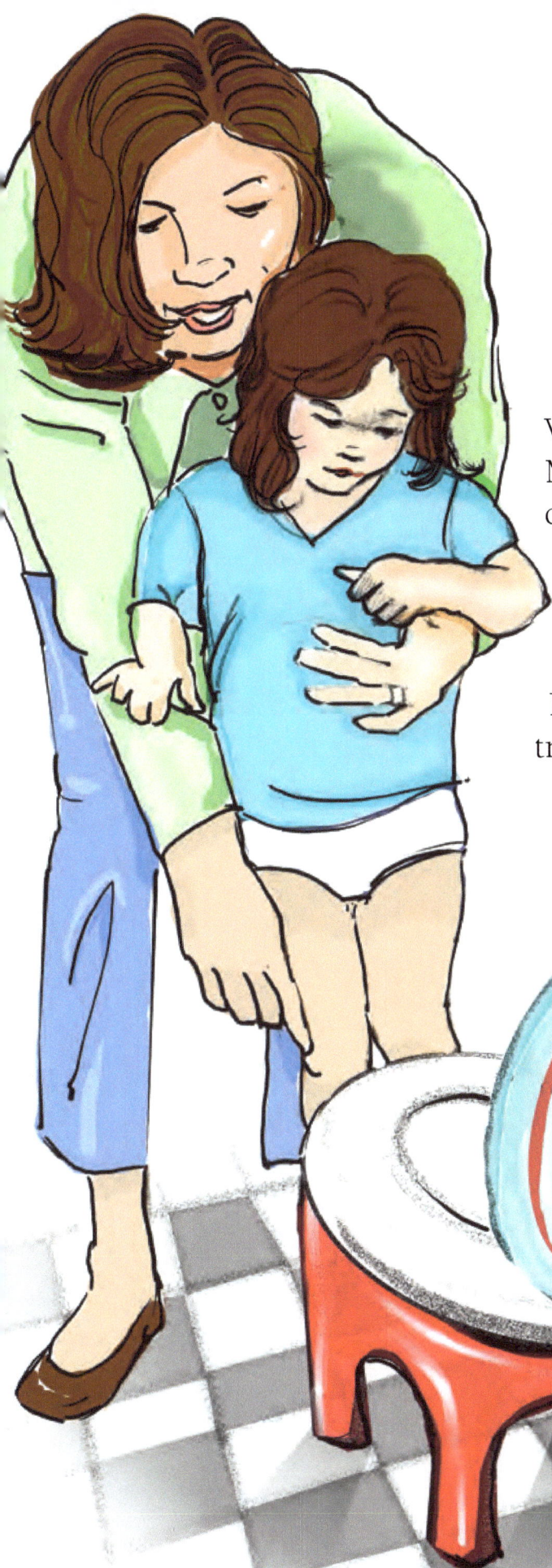

When Alexa's
Mommy brought
out her new
POTTY CHAIR
Alexa suddenly had a
great idea.

Her dolly Kelly could
try it out first!

*Kelly liked
sitting
on the potty!*

So she sat Kelly on the potty, and she just sat there and smiled.

When Alexa decided she was all done, she gave Kelly a big hug and said, "You did such a good job!"

Then all of a sudden Alexa had to go potty.

What should she do?

Should she try out her new potty or
just use her diapers like always before??

"If Kelly can use the potty, then so can I," thought Alexa.

So she pulled down her pants and tried to take off her diapers while calling out, "Mommy, I'm going potty!"

Oops ...
I took too long.

She didn't quite make it to the potty.
"Oops ..." said Alexa. "I guess I took too long."

Her mommy smiled and said, "That's ok, honey. I'm glad you gave it a try."

Alexa knew that the next time she was going to make it.

Then Alexa took a nap and when she woke up, she had to go potty again!

She jumped out of bed and ran to the bathroom.

Her mommy met her there and together they pulled off her diapers, and she sat down for the first time on her potty. She wondered what it would be like and all of a sudden, she realized that she had just gone potty in her potty chair!

She did it! She really did it!

She giggled with excitement!

Her mommy gave her a big hug and said, "I'm so proud of you, Alexa!"

She did it!
She really
did it!

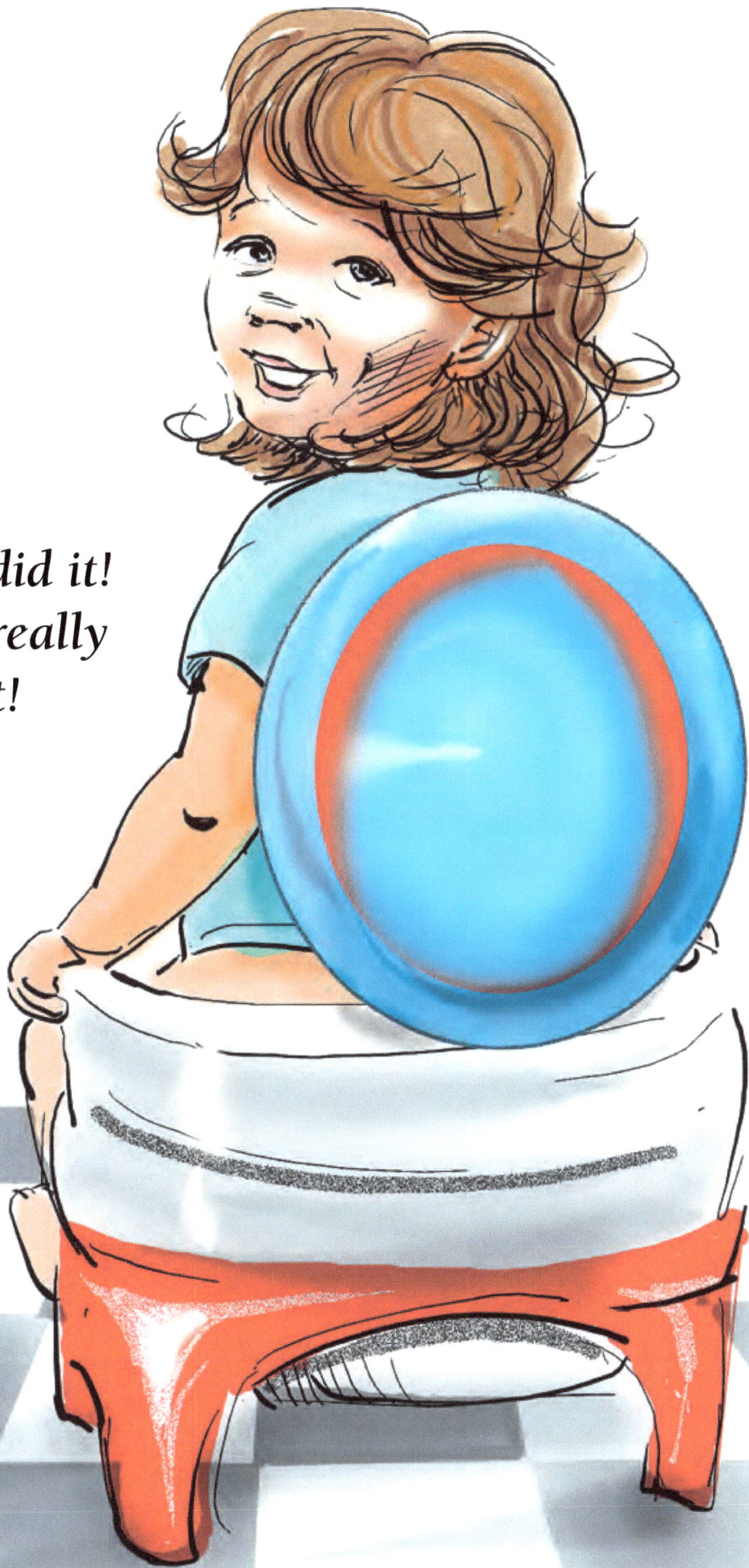

Later that day, Alexa brought all her dollies and stuffed
animals into the bathroom to show them her new potty chair.

They all seemed to like it and Alexa just knew
that they wished they had their own potty too.

Alexa couldn't wait to tell her daddy all about her
new experience that day. She knew that he would be
so happy for her.

I'm having fun!

Alexa remembered that her daddy liked to read when he was on the big people's potty …
he said it was "relaxing" … whatever that means!

So she got all her favorite books and laid them next to her potty chair.

When Alexa sat on the potty chair for the second time, she opened up her mommy's book on "Potty Training Your Child."

She sat back and started to read it and just then her mommy walked in and smiled and said, "Are you learning anything new, Alexa?!"

Alexa giggled.

Now she was looking grown up just like the kids in the book.

Over the next few days, Alexa did
such a good job using her potty
chair, that her mommy said,
"Let's go shopping and buy you
some special underwear!"

What fun that was!
There were so many pretty ones
to choose from.

After looking at them all, Alexa
chose a pair with sparkly
rainbows and teddy bears with
bows.

She couldn't wait to get home and
try them on!

*It feels BIG
up here!*

Alexa was still wearing diapers at night and one day she
asked her mommy if she could use the "big people's" potty.

Her mommy said that would be ok.

At first when Alexa sat on it, it felt so big!

Her feet stuck up in the air,

and she had to hold on tight!

She wondered how she was going to get
toilet paper and hold on at the same time.
But sure enough she was able to do it,
and felt very happy about this new accomplishment.

She felt like such a big girl!
Potty training really is fun!

Yay! You went potty!

Her mommy and daddy were always so HAPPY when she went potty.

She kind of wondered why they got so excited about her potty, but as you know,

grownups are
kind of
FuNny sometimes.

Oh no!

I'm **not** going to try **THAT** again.

One day while Alexa was on the "big people's" potty, she thought it would be fun to make designs with the toilet paper and to pretend that she was wrapping a boo-boo on her arm.

She swirled the paper on the floor and then twisted it around and around her arm. She was having so much fun until she ran out of toilet paper. So she unwrapped herself and picked up the rest of the toilet paper on the floor and flushed it down the toilet.

"Oh no!" thought Alexa as she watched the water slowly rise to the top.

Her mommy came to her rescue and stuck this funny looking rubber thing with a stick on it (her mommy called it a plunger) and bounced up and down and up and down and up and down!

Alexa giggled
as she watched
her mommy.

Finally the water
in the toilet went D
                    O
                    W
                    N

and Alexa
decided *NOT* to do that again!

Later that day, Alexa thought it would be fun to use the potty like her big brother. So she lifted the seat on the toilet and stood facing it, and while standing on her tippy toes, she went potty …
just like she'd seen her brother do.

"Yikes!" Alexa thought as she realized that she hadn't even hit the potty.

Her mommy put her in the tub to clean up and Alexa knew that she would **NOT** try **THAT** again either! How did her big brother do it?

"*Sitting* on the potty works much better for me!" thought Alexa.

Watch out
for the
germ bugs!

It seemed that whenever Alexa went shopping with her mommy or rode in the car, she had to go potty.

Then her mommy would
       hurry to get her to a bathroom.

It was kind of different when they went to these bathrooms, because her mommy would cover the toilet seat with paper and not let her touch anything.

She said these bathrooms had lots of germs …

Alexa didn't know what those were, but she figured they must be bugs or something.

Alexa called these bathrooms the *"hurry up and go!"* bathrooms.

One morning Alexa's mommy said, "You've done such a good job using the potty during the day, and now it's time to work on not wearing diapers at night."

Alexa wasn't sure about this … how would she know if she had to go potty while she was sleeping?!

But her mommy said, "I know you can do this, Alexa, and to make it more fun, if you go seven nights without going in your diapers, we'll all celebrate by having a big Potty Training Party with cake and games. It'll be your Special Day!"

Alexa thought that sounded like fun, so she decided to give it her best try.

She said to her mommy and daddy, "When I am able to wear my undies to bed at night, then we'll be the Underwear Family!"

They all laughed, and Alexa giggled just thinking about it!

Alexa's mommy got out a calendar and together they counted out the seven nights on the calendar … 1 … 2 … 3 … 4 … 5 … 6 … and 7.

The seventh night was Friday.

Alexa was so excited when she went to bed that night! As she laid down, she prayed, "Dear God, thank you for mommy, daddy, and my big brother, Ben. And, God, please help me to do good tonight and not go potty in my diapers. I am ready to be a big girl now, AND I'll get to have cake and a party just for me. I love You. Amen."

Dear God,
help me
do good.

When Alexa woke up the next morning,
she ran to her parents room and said,

"Check my diapers!! Did I make it?

Did I make it?"

And she *had*! She shouted with joy,
"YIPPEE!"

Now she only had **six** nights to go.
She just knew she could do it!

Even her big brother cheered her on …
probably because he wanted some cake … but that was ok.
It still made her feel good.

Could she do it?

The next night,

and the next night,

and the next night,

and the next night,

    and the next night after that

    Alexa did not go potty in her diapers.

Finally it was Friday night … the last night.

Alexa was very excited because tomorrow was going to be her special day … her day of celebration with cake and games, and all she had to do was make it though the night without going in her diapers.

Could she do it?

As Alexa went to bed that night, she felt a little tingle in her tummy, because it meant so much to her to be potty trained, and most of all, because she wanted to become a big girl and celebrate with a party and cake!

She then prayed, "Dear God, thank You for helping me to do good, and now tonight is my last night. Please help me not to go potty in my diapers. I know that I can do it with Your help.

I love you and mommy and daddy and my brother … and You're invited to my party, too!"

    She finally

        drifted off

            to sleep.

As the sun shone through her window the next morning, Alexa opened her eyes and suddenly remembered that TODAY was THE DAY!

She excitedly hopped out of bed … she was almost afraid to look … but then she just KNEW she did it!

She turned to the door to run and tell Mommy and Daddy and then she stopped.

Her eyes grew big…

Hanging from her doorway were rainbow colored
s t r e a m e r s and a

HUGE SIGN with colorful letters:

HAPPY POTTY DAY!

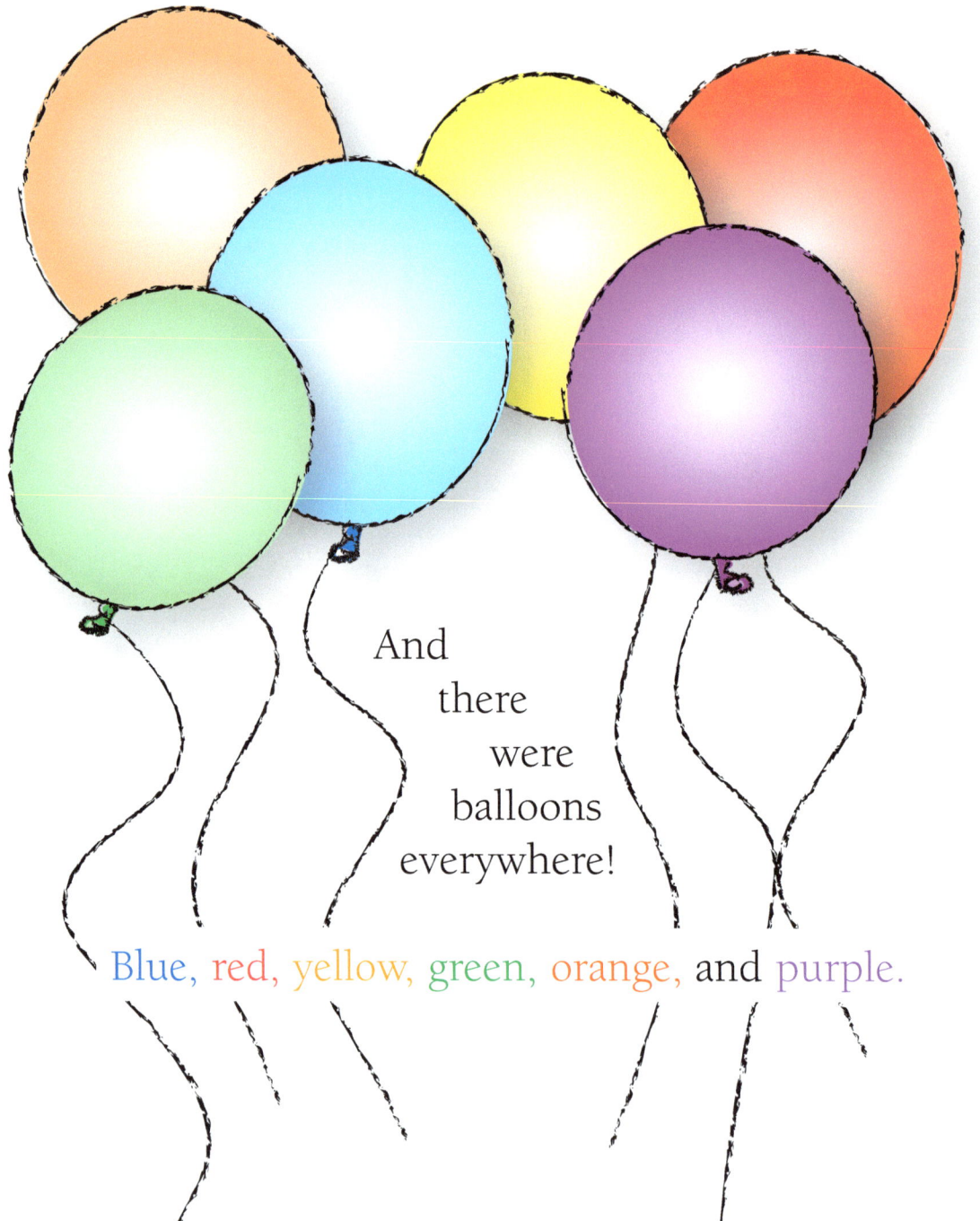

And
there
were
balloons
everywhere!

Blue, red, yellow, green, orange, and purple.

Alexa walked into the family roon and saw MORE
balloons and a big banner over the fireplace.

Her mommy and daddy came running out of the kitchen
and gave her a big hug and kiss and told her how proud
they were of her. They just knew that she would do it!

Her mommy told her that the banner said,

"Happy Potty Training Day, Alexa!
Congratulations!"

What a wonderful day this was for Alexa!
No more diapers!
She felt so SPECIAL and *knew* that she was
a big girl now!

Later that day, her mommy brought out Alexa's favorite cake
mix and they made it together for her celebration party.

They mixed it,

and they baked it,

and they frosted it with yummy purple

frosting because it was Alexa's

favorite color!

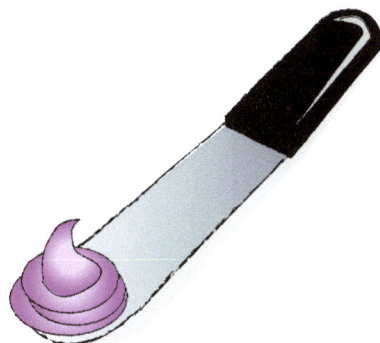

Alexa LOVED helping her mommy make cakes!

Her Daddy said, "Alexa, you can choose your favorite place to eat for lunch!"

Alexa thought for a minute—
It was so hard to choose!
She liked chicken. She like hamburgers. She liked tacos.

But, her favoirte food was PIZZA!

So Daddy and Mommy said, "Let's go!"

Alexa thought this special event meant she should dress up.

She put on her best purple dress with the pink collar and sash and big shiny buttons.

While they were at the pizza parlor, she told Mommy she needed to use the bathroom.

Mommy walked with her to the restroom, and as Alexa passed some other kids at another table, she smiled to herself and thought, "I'm on my way to the bathroom because I'm POTTY TRAINED!"

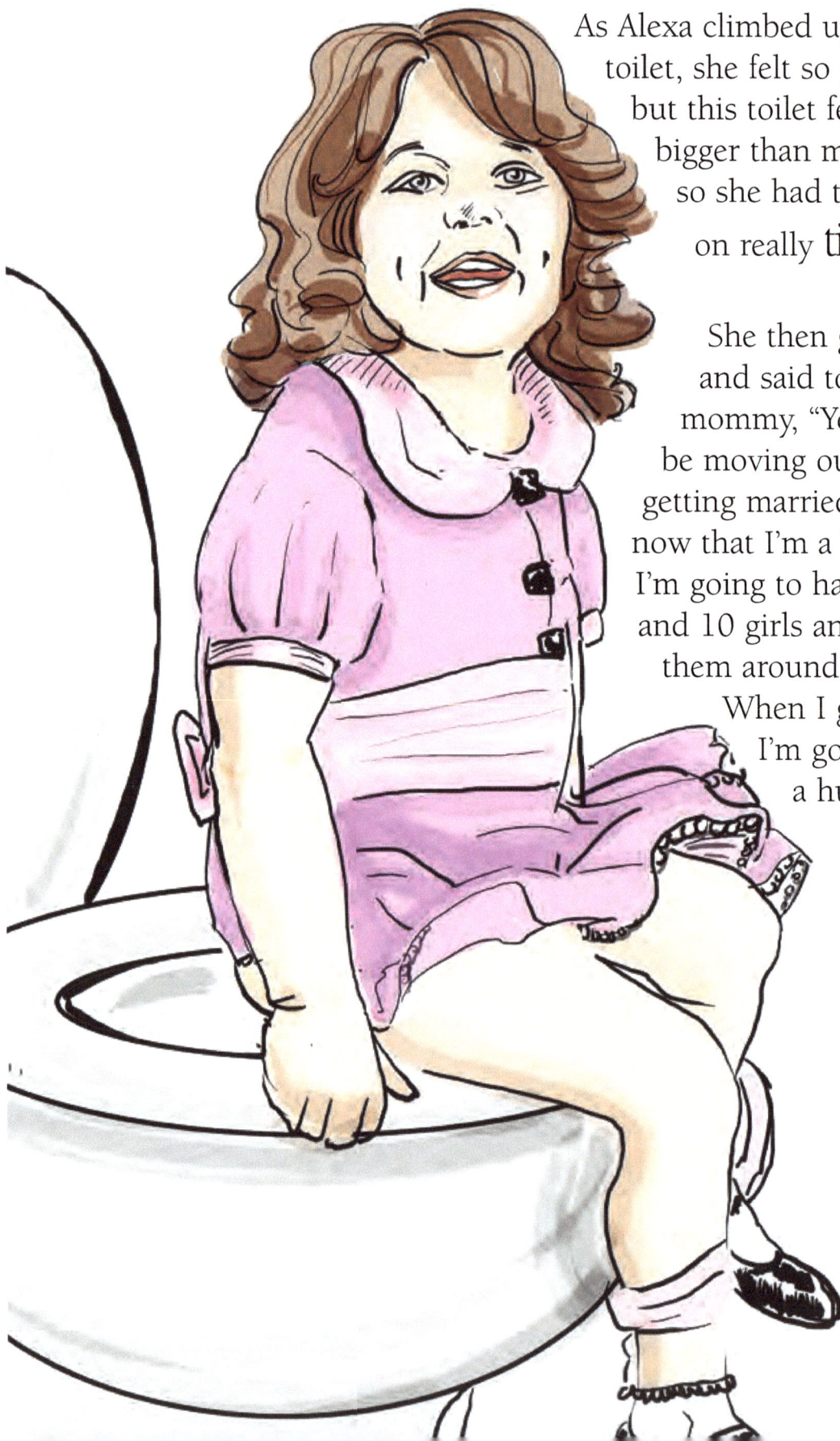

As Alexa climbed up on the
toilet, she felt so grown up—
but this toilet felt
bigger than most,
so she had to hold
on really tight.

She then giggled
and said to her
mommy, "You know, I'll
be moving out soon and
getting married,
now that I'm a big girl.
I'm going to have 10 boys
and 10 girls and drive
them around in a bus.
When I get married,
I'm going to have
a huge cake!"

She then thought for a moment and asked her mommy,
"Is that why you got married, so you could
have a big cake?"

Her mommy just smiled and a tear came to her eye,
because she knew that all too soon
her little Alexa would be all grown up.

This was just the start of many exciting
changes in her little girl's life.

After lunch the whole family went to the toy store. Alexa looked at all there was, but finally chose a new dolly...her other dollies would have a new friend!

When they got home, her Mommy and Daddy put some candles on the cake and lit them, and they all sang

"Happy Potty Training to You …
Happy Potty Training to You …
Happy Potty Training, Dear Alexa,
Happy Potty Training to You!"

Alexa blew out the candles, ate the cake, and together they played games and tossed around the balloons.

That night, Alexa's mommy put on her pajamas and for the first time, she wore her underwear to bed. They were so much more comfortable than diapers.

Alexa excitedly shouted out,
"Now we're the Underwear Family! Yippee!"

As Alexa lay down in her cozy bed, she thought about the wonderful day she had and how special everyone had made her feel. She then prayed, "Thank You so much, God, for helping me to become a big girl. I love You so much.

"Oh, and I saved You some cake!"

She just knew that God was smiling down at her and saying, "Good job, Alexa! I was with you every step of the way, and I knew you could do it! I love YOU, too."

She snuggled her new dolly and stretched out to go to sleep.

To her surprise, she felt her toes touch the end of her bed, and she knew that today, on this special day, she had GROWN even bigger.

www.ingramcontent.com/pod-product-compliance
Lightning Source LLC
Chambersburg PA
CBHW041220040426

42443CB00002B/26